TIMELINES

The Struggle Against Apartheid

Patience Coster

ARCTURUS

This edition first published in 2010 by Arcturus Publishing
Distributed by Black Rabbit Books
P.O. Box 3263
Mankato
Minnesota MN 56002

Printed in China

Library of Congress Cataloging-in-Publication Data

Coster, Patience.
　The struggle against apartheid / Patience Coster.
　　　p. cm. -- (Timelines)
　Includes index.
　Summary: "Discusses events in South Africa that lead up to and followed the
end of apartheid, beginning with the peace treaty of Vereeniging and continuing
through the election of Jacob Zuma"--Provided by publisher.
　ISBN 978-1-84837-640-3 (library bound)
　1. Apartheid--South Africa--History--Juvenile literature. 2. South Africa--Race
relations--Juvenile literature. 3. South Africa--History--20th century--Juvenile
literature. I. Title.
　DT1757.C673 2011
　305.800968'0904--dc22
　　　　　　　　　　　　　　　　　2009051269

Series concept: Alex Woolf
Editor and picture researcher: Cath Senker
Consultant: James Vaughan
Designer: Ariadne Ward
Cartography: The map on page 6 is by Stefan Chabluk.

Picture Credits:
Bridgeman Art Library: 4. Corbis: cover (africanpictures/akg-images), 5 (Hulton-Deutsch Collection),
6 (Hulton-Deutsch Collection), 9 (Bettmann), 10, 11, 12 (Bettmann), 14 (Bettmann), 15 (Bettmann),
16 (Bettmann), 17 (Hulton-Deutsch Collection), 18 (Bettmann), 20 (Jon Hrusa/epa), 22 (Bettmann),
26 (Bettmann), 29 (Jon Jones/Sygma), 30 (Hulton-Deutsch Collection), 31 (Bettmann), 32 Selwyn Tait/Sygma),
34 (Bettmann), 35 (Kevin Carter/Megan Patricia Carter Trust/Sygma), 36 (Bernard Bisson/Sygma), 37 (William
Campbell/Sygma), 38 (David Turnley), 39 (Richard Olivier), 41 (Greg Marinovich/Sygma), 42 (Peter
Andrews/Reuters), 44 above (Peter Andrews/Reuters), 44 below (Gideon Mendel). Getty Images: 13 (FPG),
19 (Terrence Spencer/Time Life Pictures), 21 (Jurgen Schadeberg), 24 (Terrence Spencer/Time Life Pictures),
25 (Express Newspapers/Archive Photos), 27 (Guy Tillim/AFP), 33 (Central Press), 40 (Alexander Joe/AFP),
43 (Jean-Pierre Muller/AFP). PA Photos: 23 (AP/Press Association Images). Rex Features: 28. University of
Witwatersrand: 8.
Cover picture: Nelson Mandela arrives at a public meeting during the election campaign of 1994.

ISBN: 978-1-84837-640-3
SL001324US
Supplier 03, Date 0210

Contents

▶ The Peace of Vereeniging: May 31, 1902 — **4**

▶ The Union of South Africa: May 31, 1910 — **6**

▶ African Opposition: January 8-12, 1912 — **8**

▶ The Natives' Land Act: June 19, 1913 — **10**

▶ The Passive Resistance Campaign: June 13, 1946 — **12**

▶ The Apartheid Election: May 26, 1948 — **14**

▶ The Bantu Authorities Act: July 17, 1951 — **16**

▶ The Defiance Campaign: April 6, 1952 — **18**

▶ The Congress of the People: June 26, 1955 — **20**

▶ Sharpeville: March 21, 1960 — **22**

▶ South Africa Leaves the Commonwealth: May 31, 1961 — **24**

▶ Mandela Sentenced to Life Imprisonment: June 12, 1964 — **26**

▶ The South African Students' Organization: July 1, 1969 — **28**

▶ The Soweto Uprising: June 16, 1976 — **30**

▶ The Death of Steve Biko: September 12, 1977 — **32**

▶ Murder in Sharpeville: September 3, 1984 — **34**

▶ State of Emergency: July 20, 1985 — **36**

▶ F. W. de Klerk Is Elected: September 14, 1989 — **38**

▶ The Release of Mandela: February 11, 1990 — **40**

▶ The First Non-racial Elections: April 27, 1994 — **42**

▶ Hopes for the Future: October 28, 1998 — **44**

▶ Key Figures in the Apartheid Era — **46**

▶ Glossary — **47**

▶ Further Information — **47**

▶ Index — **48**

The Peace of Vereeniging

MAY 31, 1902

On May 31, 1902, the governments of the British and Boer republics in South Africa signed a peace treaty at Melrose House in Pretoria. Known as the Peace of Vereeniging, this settlement marked the end of a war that had been raging in South Africa since 1899.

COLONIZING THE LAND

The descendants of Dutch farmers, the Boers, or Afrikaners, had made their home in South Africa during the 17th century. British interests in the country dated back to 1795, when Britain took over the Cape of Good Hope area as a stopping-off point for its ships traveling to and from colonies in Australia and India.

Throughout the 19th century, tensions between British colonists and Boer settlers ran high, but the discovery of diamonds in the Orange River valley (in 1867) and gold in the Transvaal (in the 1870s) brought matters to a head. The First Boer War (1880–1881) and the Second Boer War (1899–1902) were fought for control of these valuable resources. British military might, combined with brutal tactics that included the imprisonment and deaths of thousands of people in concentration camps, resulted in the eventual surrender of the Boers.

Between the hours of 7 & 8 a.m. the Boer Prisoners are expected to perform their ablutions

Under the Peace of Vereeniging, the Boers were promised the release of their prisoners of war, the limited protection of their language in court and schools, the right to keep firearms, the right to own property, and eventual political independence. A further promise was the continued restriction of the rights of the black peoples of South Africa.

A British illustration from 1900 shows Boer prisoners of war lining up to wash. However, the reality was much harsher than this colorful scene suggests. Between 20,000 and 26,000 Boers, many of them women and children, died of disease and hunger in the concentration camps.

Scorched-earth policy

"Whenever the enemy now appears, he carries out indescribable destruction. All houses are burned down, all fields and gardens utterly destroyed, all cattle and foodstuffs carried off, and all males taken prisoner!"
Boer general Jan Smuts, "Memoir of the Boer War", September 22, 1900.
Quoted in T. R. H. Davenport, *South Africa: A Modern History* (Macmillan, 1992).

TIMELINE	**AMBITIONS OF EMPIRE, 1652–1902**
1652	▶ Dutch colonists settle at the Cape.
1867	▶ Diamonds are discovered near the Orange River.
Jan.–Aug. 1879	▶ British defeat the Zulus in the Zulu War.
Dec. 16, 1880–Feb. 27, 1881	▶ First Boer War.
1880–1900	▶ Imperial powers compete to gain control of land and resources in southern Africa.
1886	▶ Discovery of gold in Witwatersrand near Johannesburg.
October 11, 1899–May 31, 1902	▶ Second Boer War.

THE ORIGINS OF APARTHEID

The idea of apartheid, meaning "apartness," or the separation of people according to the color of their skin, is rooted in the history of human migration to southern Africa. For thousands of years, many black peoples lived there. When white Europeans arrived, with their superior weapons, they gained control of the land, generally at the expense of the majority black population. The 19th-century boom in mining relied on black labor together with workers brought from India and China. Social and racial distinctions were clearly drawn—white people governed and non-whites served.

This photograph from 1888 shows workers at the entrance to a diamond mine. To combat the theft of diamonds, the British mine owners said that black workers had to live in compounds and carry identity papers, known as passbooks.

CROSS-REFERENCE APARTHEID LAWS: PAGES 14–15, 16–17 ▶

The Union of South Africa

MAY 31, 1910

On May 31, 1910, the British gave the four colonies of Transvaal, the Orange Free State, Natal, and the Cape of Good Hope self-rule as the Union of South Africa. Britain was anxious to satisfy the Afrikaner desire for self-government and create a unified country in its empire. The union split control of the country between the British and the Afrikaners, leaving the black population with few rights.

VESTED INTERESTS

The Afrikaners saw themselves as frontierspeople who had tamed the land. Afrikaner culture produced a strong sense of national identity and

This map of South Africa under apartheid indicates the borders established by the 1910 Union and shows the places mentioned in this book.

resistance to change. On the other hand, British interests in South Africa were based on trade and ideas of empire. During the 19th century, increasing British control had resulted in the introduction of English laws and language, much to the anger of the Afrikaners. By the start of the 20th century, Afrikaner resentment toward the British had become intense.

An Afrikaner family group from the Transvaal, photographed in the early 1900s. The Afrikaners saw themselves as a nation and demanded absolute power in what they believed to be their own state.

SHAPING A WHITE DOMINION, 1902–1911

1905 ▶ The South African Native Affairs Commission proposes separate territories for black and white people.

1906 ▶ A rebellion in Zululand is put down by the British.

March 22, 1907 ▶ The Transvaal Registration Act requires people of Indian descent to carry passbooks containing their fingerprints so that the authorities can control their movements (pass laws already apply to Africans).

May 31, 1910 ▶ The Union of South Africa takes away political rights of black people.

1911 ▶ The Mines and Works Act reserves certain skilled positions for white and Colored (of mixed race) people only.

A white frame of mind

"All the Afrikaner had to assert his superiority was his white skin, his racial status symbol. It made his whiteness the most supremely important thing, all that prevented him from sinking to the very bottom, and the maintenance of racial distinctions a compelling necessity."
Allister Sparks, *The Mind of South Africa: The Story of the Rise and Fall of Apartheid* (Heinemann, 1990).

BRITISH CONTROL

Following the Boer defeat in 1902, the British governor of the Cape, Lord Alfred Milner, had full control of South African affairs. He encouraged British immigration in the hope that English-speaking white people would dominate the country politically. Yet his plan to anglicize the country failed, and the new Liberal government in Britain from 1906 sought to win Afrikaner cooperation. Afrikaner leader Jan Smuts lobbied the British for self-government in the Transvaal, pressing for a united South Africa in which English and Dutch speakers would bury their differences. His efforts resulted in the Union of South Africa, with the former Boer leader, General Louis Botha, as prime minister. The constitution removed the voting rights of non-white property owners and laid the foundations for an apartheid state.

CROSS-REFERENCE NATIVES' LAND ACT: PAGES 10–11

African Opposition

Members of the South African Native National Convention (SANNC) visited Britain in 1914 to protest against the 1913 Natives' Land Act.

Between January 8 and 12, 1912, African chiefs, representatives of people's and church organizations, and other prominent individuals gathered in Bloemfontein in the Orange Free State to plan a campaign against their political exclusion and the tightening of controls over their daily lives. At this conference they formed the South African Native National Convention (SANNC). Renamed the African National Congress (ANC) in 1923, its aim was to bring all Africans together to defend their rights.

DISCRIMINATION

During the 19th century, whites had defeated South African blacks in wars and exploited them during peacetime. They introduced pass laws to restrict the movement of Africans; all black people had to carry documents showing they were allowed to be in a certain area. Under the Union of 1910, their political rights were denied. No non-white person was allowed to sit as a representative in the South African parliament. Black, Indian, and Colored people

No voice

"The white people of this country have formed what is known as the Union of South Africa – a union in which we have no voice in the making of laws and no part in their administration. We have called you therefore to this conference so that we can together devise ways and means of forming our national union for the purpose of creating national unity and defending our rights."
Zulu lawyer Pixley ka Izaka Seme, speaking at Bloemfontein, 1912.

TIMELINE

1910s–1930s ▶

1913 ▶

May 1918 ▶

1919 ▶

1920 ▶

December 1921 ▶

EARLY PROTESTS, 1910s–1930s

Africans educated at missionary schools attempt to organize to resist white rule and gain political power. Their efforts are weakened because few Africans can read and write, communication is poor, and access to money or other resources is limited.

Black women organize peaceful protests against pass laws.

A strike for a pay increase by "night soil boys" (sanitation workers) in Johannesburg triggers a succession of strikes by black workers.

The Industrial and Commercial Union is founded.

The SANNC supports a strike by African mine workers.

The South African Communist Party (SACP) calls for a pass-burning campaign.

could only vote in Union elections in the Cape. In 1912, groups representing Indians (the Indian Congress of Natal) and Coloured people (the African Political Organization of Cape Coloureds) established links with the SANNC to protest against these restrictions.

NO JUSTICE

The original members of the SANNC believed that the British government would treat them fairly. However, any possibility of justice was overruled by Britain's interests in the gold mines and by the need for black labor. A visit by a group of SANNC members to London to protest against the Natives' Land Act of 1913 was ignored. Many black people felt that direct action, in the form of strikes and protests such as passbook burning, was the only way to draw attention to their situation.

CROSS-REFERENCE
NATIVES' LAND
ACT: PAGES 10–11
ANC: PAGES
18–19, 40–41,
44–45

White as well as African mine workers went on strike in the early 20th century, angry about high death rates and the introduction of foreign labor. In this photo from the 1910s, they are gathering at a strike meeting in Johannesburg.

The Natives' Land Act

On June 19, 1913, the South African parliament passed the Natives' Land Act. This law set aside 7.3 percent of the land for reserves in which the country's population of 5.5 million black people were expected to live. The remaining 92.7 percent of the land, which included the most productive regions and the major towns, was allocated to the population of 1.5 million whites. The Natives' Land Act was an important step toward establishing segregation throughout South Africa.

BLACK LABOR

At the start of the 20th century, white farmers relied on African laborers to tend the land. In terms of industry, South Africa's mineral wealth was of huge importance to the British. Transvaal was the world's largest single producer of gold, and the British-owned mining companies needed cheap labor to extract and crush the ore. For their own convenience, the companies housed their African workers in compounds near the mines.

However, given the choice, Africans rejected the backbreaking toil of mining and started moving into towns to search for other work. This threatened the ability of whites to keep themselves separate. The Natives' Land Act banned the selling of white-owned land to black people

African miners take their "rest hour" in a compound at a South African diamond mine, 1901.

Allocation of land under the Natives' Land Act

	Total area	Black reserves	% of land for black people
	in morgen—about 2 acres (0.8 hectare)		
Cape	83,700,000	6,217,037	7.5
Transvaal	33,400,000	1,159,296	3.5
Natal	10,650,000	2,972,312	29.7
Orange Free State	14,800,000	74,290	0.5

Source: *Apartheid: A History*, Brian Lapping (Grafton Books, 1986).

TIMELINE

AFRIKANER NATIONALISM ON THE RISE, 1914–1924

July 1, 1914 ▶ Hard-line Afrikaner J. B. M. Hertzog founds the National Party.

July 26, 1915 ▶ *Die Burger* newspaper is set up to represent the views of the National Party, with Daniel Malan as editor.

1923 ▶ The Native Urban Areas Act gives the authorities control over the movement of the black population in towns and cities. Urban local authorities are required to provide segregated locations or townships for non-whites.

April 8, 1924 ▶ The Industrial Conciliation Act excludes Africans from membership in registered trade unions and bans black trade unions.

June 1924 ▶ The National Party wins the general election and Hertzog becomes prime minister.

and forced blacks to live in reserves. This meant that the whites, who made up less than a quarter of the total population, owned almost all the land in South Africa. Black people were only allowed into white areas when they were needed as workers.

AN ANGRY PEOPLE

Despite the laws that favored whites, the Afrikaner population was still at a disadvantage compared to English-speaking whites. In 1914, the National Party was formed to fight for the interests of the Afrikaner population.

In Durban in the early 20th century, rickshaw drivers pose for a photo wearing traditional headdresses. The segregation of residential areas in cities meant that workers like these were housed in locations on the edge of town.

CROSS-REFERENCE UNION OF SOUTH AFRICA: PAGES 6–7 BANTUSTANS: PAGES 16–17 ▶

The Passive Resistance Campaign

On June 13, 1946, a campaign of passive (non-violent) resistance was launched by the Natal Indian Congress (NIC) to protest against government restrictions on the rights of Indians to own or occupy land in Natal. A mass meeting of more than 15,000 people in Durban was followed by a march. At the end, 17 resisters pitched tents on a street corner in defiance of what they called the "Ghetto Act". Despite physical attacks from white people, during which an Indian plainclothes policeman was killed, the resisters remained in their temporary camp until June 27.

GANDHI

Since the 1880s, various resistance organizations had sprung up among the non-white population. The first one to make a real impact was founded by Mohandas K. Gandhi, an Indian lawyer. Gandhi arrived in South Africa in 1893 to provide legal services to Indian businessmen in Natal but soon found himself at the center of a segregation debate. The British government had introduced a law requiring Indians to carry passes in Natal (a similar law was later brought into effect in the Transvaal in 1907).

Gandhi used techniques of non-violent resistance (*satyagraha*, or "soul force"), which involved not complying with the law and being imprisoned, if necessary, to register his opposition to this discrimination against the Indian population.

USING SOUL FORCE

In 1946, when the white population of Natal tried to prevent Indians from owning land in "white" areas,

JUNE 13, 1946

Mohandas Gandhi (seated, center) and his associates pose outside their law offices in Johannesburg in about 1895.

CROSS-REFERENCE
DEFIANCE
CAMPAIGN:
PAGES 18–19

TIMELINE

EARLY DAYS IN THE STRUGGLE, 1944–1948

1944 ▶ The ANC Youth League is formed. Its members include Robert Sobukwe, Nelson Mandela, Walter Sisulu, and Oliver Tambo.

June 6, 1946 ▶ The Asiatic Land Tenure and Indian Representation Act (also known as the "Ghetto Act") restricts the rights of Indians to own or occupy land.

1946–48 ▶ Indian Passive Resistance Campaign takes place.

August 15, 1947 ▶ In India, Gandhi helps to achieve Indian independence from British rule.

protesters followed Gandhi's example. The ANC would later adopt his policy of non-violent resistance in many of its protests. It was a form of action that tested the ability, skills, and determination of the people to sustain a campaign in which they came into direct conflict with the authorities.

Civil rights campaigner G. M. Naicker, president of the Natal Indian Congress, addresses a group of demonstrators during the protest against the "Ghetto Act" in 1946.

We shall resist!

"The brutal assault on myself and my fellow resisters are signs of the weakness of our oppressors. We may be harmed and physically maimed or even die, but the spirit of our people will not die because of these brutal and cowardly attacks. In the face of all WE SHALL RESIST." Rabia Docrat, one of the passive resisters who was injured during the 1946 campaign. Quoted in www.anc.org.za/ancdocs/history/congress/passive.html .

The Apartheid Election

MAY 26, 1948

Under the apartheid laws, status was determined by the color of people's skin, with whites at the top, Africans at the bottom, and Indian people in between. This caused inter-racial tensions that boiled over into race riots between African and Indian people in Durban in 1949.

On May 26, 1948, an Afrikaner-only government was elected in South Africa. The new prime minister, ex-clergyman Daniel Malan, believed that Afrikaners were God's chosen people. He saw them as disadvantaged by centuries of British oppression and worked to ensure that South Africa broke its remaining links with the British empire. The way he went about asserting Afrikaner dominance would have a disastrous effect on South Africa's black population.

RACIST LEGISLATION

With just a slim majority in government, Malan set about securing a future for his people by making apartheid into an official system to control relations between blacks and whites. A steady stream of laws was passed that extended racial discrimination. The Prohibition of Mixed Marriages Act (1949) and the Immorality Act (1950) extended the existing ban on sex between black and white people to prohibit sex between whites and all other non-white South Africans. The Population Registration Act (1950) divided people into

TIMELINE

APARTHEID LAWS, 1927–1950

September 30, 1927 ▸ Sexual relations between blacks and whites are banned.

July 10, 1936 ▸ The Representation of Natives Act removes black voters from the Cape electoral roll and sets up a separate electoral roll for them. They can vote only for white representatives.

January 1949 ▸ Race riots occur in Durban between Africans and Indians.

July 8, 1949 ▸ Marriages between whites and members of other racial groups are prohibited.

July 7, 1950 ▸ The Population Registration Act divides people into four racial groups.

July 7, 1950 ▸ The Group Areas Act forces people to live in an area designated for their racial category.

four racial categories: white, Coloured (mixed race), "Asiatic" (Indian) and "Native" (later "Bantu" or African). At the same time, the Group Areas Act (1950) established segregated areas in towns and cities for each racial group, forcing many people to leave their homes and relocate.

Prime Minister Daniel Malan fought for the rights of Afrikaners and, in doing so, introduced laws to limit the rights of non-white peoples.

Inequality and resistance

- By 1939, fewer than 30 percent of Africans were receiving any formal education, and whites were earning over five times as much as Africans.
- White mine workers were paid 12 times more than their African counterparts, even though Africans were forced to do the most dangerous jobs.
- In 1946, over 75,000 Africans went on strike in support of higher wages.

CROSS-REFERENCE ORIGINS OF APARTHEID: PAGES 4–5, 6–7 BANTU AUTHORITIES ACT: PAGES 16–17

The Bantu Authorities Act

JULY 17, 1951

On July 17, 1951, the Bantu Authorities Act came into force. It was a government measure designed to restrict the black population to specific "tribal" areas. "Bantu" was the name given to the group of languages spoken by almost all people living in southern Africa. It came to be used by whites as a racist term for black Africans generally. The act designated the lands reserved for black Africans as independent nations or Bantustans (homelands). For example, the Transkei Bantustan was assigned to the Xhosa-speaking people who came from that area.

STRIPPED OF CITIZENSHIP

The Group Areas Act (1950) had ensured that the best areas and most of the land were reserved for the white population. Now the government stripped millions of black people of their South African citizenship and forced them to become residents of the new Bantustans. Africans were to be considered foreigners in white-controlled South Africa. They needed passbooks to go there and were admitted only to serve whites in menial jobs. Gradually, non-white guest workers began to settle in squatter camps on the edge of cities to be closer to their place of work.

EDUCATION

Hendrik Verwoerd had been appointed Minister of Native Affairs in 1950. Verwoerd was even more determined than Malan to make

The final day of class in a mission school, which closed down in protest against the Bantu Education Act of 1953. The people running the school felt they would not be able to teach children satisfactorily under the apartheid system.

TIMELINE

TOTAL APARTHEID, 1951–1959

July 6, 1951 ▶ The Prevention of Illegal Squatting Act forces Africans to move off public or privately owned land. Local authorities are permitted to set up resettlement camps where squatters can be concentrated.

July 17, 1951 ▶ The Bantu Authorities Act is passed.

January 1, 1954 ▶ The Bantu Education Act of 1953 comes into force.

June 19, 1959 ▶ The Promotion of Bantu Self-Government Act provides for the founding of eight Bantustans with powers to tax their own people and control local affairs.

apartheid work. In 1953, his Bantu Education Act gave the government control of African education. Before, missionaries had run African schools, but many Afrikaners considered these schools to be too independent. The Department of Native Affairs now supervised the education of all Africans, yet it provided far fewer resources than for white education. Non-whites were no longer allowed to attend white universities.

CROSS-REFERENCE NATIVES' LAND ACT PAGES: 10–11 APARTHEID LAWS: PAGES 14–15

In London in the 1950s, anti-apartheid groups protest against the South African government.

Bantu segregation

"My department's policy is that Bantu education should stand with both feet in the reserves and have its roots in the spirit and being of Bantu society . . . There is no place for [the Bantu] in the European community above the level of certain forms of labour . . . What is the use of teaching the Bantu child mathematics when it cannot use it in practice? That is quite absurd."
Hendrik Verwoerd, Minister of Native Affairs, 1953. Quoted in Brian Lapping, *Apartheid: A History* (Grafton Books, 1986).

The Defiance Campaign

African protesters give the thumbs-up as they take over a railway compartment reserved for "Europeans only" as part of the Defiance Campaign in 1952.

On April 6, 1952, the ANC organized its first mass action, a campaign "for the defiance of unjust laws." ANC members had written to Daniel Malan asking him to repeal the pass laws, the Group Areas Act, and the Bantu Authorities Act. Their request had been refused outright. The 7,000 members of the ANC therefore began instructing supporters to defy the laws, which usually resulted in arrest.

PASS LAWS

The Abolition of Passes Act of 1952 was deceptively named. In place of passes, all Africans were required to carry identification booklets with their names, addresses, fingerprints, and other information. This was, in effect, a stricter type of passbook. Africans were frequently stopped and harassed for their passes. Between 1948 and 1973, more than 10 million Africans would be arrested because their passes were "not in order." Burning passbooks became a common form of protest.

DEFIANCE

The objective of the 1952 Defiance Campaign was to embarrass the government and overcrowd the prisons. The campaign received widespread support, including that of Natal Indians, white communists, and "Cape Coloureds." ANC leaders urged the use of boycotts, strikes, civil disobedience, and non-cooperation.

TIMELINE

REPRESSIVE MEASURES, 1950–1953

June 26, 1950 ▶ The Suppression of Communism Act bans the Communist Party and defines any opposition to the government as communism. It allows the government to arrest anyone it believes to be promoting communism.

July 11, 1952 ▶ The Abolition of Passes and Coordination of Documents Act comes into force.

October 9, 1953 ▶ The Preservation of Separate Amenities Act establishes "separate but not necessarily equal" parks, beaches, post offices, and other public places for whites and non-whites.

Protesters burn their passbooks as an act of defiance.

They encouraged people to throw away their passes. Nelson Mandela and 52 other men were arrested simply for walking through the streets of central Johannesburg, a white area, after 11 p.m. Likewise, groups of Africans were arrested for walking through the "Europeans Only" entrances of railway stations. By the end of 1952 and after 8,326 arrests, the campaign petered out.

CROSS-REFERENCE PASSIVE RESISTANCE CAMPAIGN: PAGES 12–13

A defining moment

"I doubt whether many of us realized at the time that the very intensity of Nationalist oppression would do what we had so far failed to achieve—wake the mass of Africans to political awareness, goad us finally out of resigned endurance."
Albert Luthuli, president general of the ANC, 1952–1967. Quoted in Brian Lapping, *Apartheid: A History* (Grafton Books, 1986).

The Congress of the People

Kliptown in 2005. In many ways, the village where the Congress of the People was held 50 years earlier has changed very little, despite the ending of apartheid.

On June 26, 1955, the African nationalist movement held the Congress of the People at Kliptown, near Johannesburg. From all over South Africa, 3,000 people gathered to draw up the Freedom Charter, which proposed a non-racial democracy with equal rights and justice for all. This marked a clear change in the anti-apartheid movement's approach. Instead of pleading for relief from government measures, the charter made positive proposals for change. It would remain the manifesto of the ANC for more than 30 years.

BANNING

Following the Defiance Campaign, the government had introduced banning orders on a number of ANC leaders, including Nelson Mandela and Albert Luthuli. These orders stopped the leaders from meeting one another, addressing their followers, or engaging in political campaigns. In 1953, some 100 activists were banned.

Demands for change

"We, the people of South Africa, declare for all our country and the world to know:
that South Africa belongs to all who live in it, black and white, and that no government can justly claim authority unless it is based on the will of all the people . . .
Every man and woman shall have the right to vote for and to stand as a candidate for all bodies which make laws . . .
There shall be equal status in the bodies of the state, in the courts, and in the schools for all national groups and races . . .
The preaching and practice of national, race, or colour discrimination and contempt shall be a punishable crime."
From the Freedom Charter, 1955.

TIMELINE

REMOVAL AND ARRESTS, 1955–1961

February 1955–1960 ▶ The black population of Sophiatown, a suburb of Johannesburg, is moved permanently to provide homes for white workers.

December 5, 1956 ▶ The government arrests 156 Congress delegates.

1956–61 ▶ The Treason Trial takes place.

March 29, 1961 ▶ All the accused are acquitted.

FIGHTING BACK

The movement fought back against these restrictions by holding the Congress of the People. The authorities arranged for police to surround the concourse and search delegates, confiscating documents. On the evidence gathered, they arrested a huge number of people, including Mandela, Luthuli, and Tambo, and put them on trial. The accused were charged with treason and with being communists. The Treason Trial was the longest and largest trial in South Africa's history. It resulted in government humiliation when, eventually, all the charges were dropped. An unexpected outcome of the trial, however, was to allow Mandela to show his remarkable abilities as a political leader and thinker.

CROSS-REFERENCE
NELSON MANDELA:
PAGES 26–27,
40–41, 42–43

Sophiatown residents wait for a truck to move them to their new homes. In 1955, using the Group Areas Act of 1950, the government moved black people from Sophiatown so that the area could be redeveloped for whites.

Sharpeville

South African police walk among the dead and dying following the Sharpeville massacre.

In 1958, Hendrik Verwoerd became prime minister. He was determined to complete his plan for a segregated South Africa by forcibly moving black communities to the Bantustans. Yet the white economy could not survive without a stable black workforce to labor in the urban areas. Black workers were therefore housed in townships on the edge of cities. One of the first townships to come to the world's attention was Sharpeville, near Vereeniging.

ANTI-PASS DAY

Some African nationalists began to feel that Africans should fight apartheid alone rather than join forces with Indians and communist whites. They broke away from the ANC to form the Pan-African Congress (PAC). The PAC announced that March 21, 1960 would be an anti-pass day, and it called on all Africans to leave their passes at home and surrender themselves to the police. A large group of Africans in the township of Sharpeville refused to carry their passes and gathered near the police station. When a scuffle broke out, the police became alarmed and opened fire, at which point people turned and fled. In all, 69 Africans were killed and 187 were wounded.

INTERNATIONAL ALARM

The Sharpeville massacre shocked people around the world. On March 30, Verwoerd declared a state of emergency and punished anti-pass demonstrators with fines, imprisonment, and whippings. The ANC and PAC were banned.

"WALLS OF GRANITE," 1955–1960

1955 ▶ Jean Sinclair founds the Black Sash, a non-violent white women's organization, to campaign against apartheid.

April 1959 ▶ The Pan-African Congress is formed.

1960 ▶ Verwoerd begins a campaign to win over English speakers to the National Party cause.

April 8, 1960 ▶ The ANC and PAC are banned following the Sharpeville massacre.

April 9, 1960 ▶ Verwoerd survives an assassination attempt by a white farmer. He tells the National Party that the South African government must stand like "walls of granite" to preserve apartheid.

A non-racial future

"It has been our aim in the countries for which we have borne responsibility to create a society . . . in which men are given the opportunity to grow to their full stature—and that must in our view include the opportunity to have an increasing share in political power and responsibility . . . Our policy therefore is non-racial. It offers a future in which Africans, Europeans, Asians . . . will all play their full part as citizens."

On February 3, 1960 British prime minister Harold Macmillan visited South Africa at the end of a tour through the African continent. He had been impressed by the strength of African nationalism and convinced that this "wind of change" blowing through the continent was irresistible. In his speech to the South African parliament, he made it clear that the apartheid policy would no longer receive support from the British government.

Quoted in Brian Lapping, *Apartheid: A History* (Grafton Books, 1986).

In Johannesburg in 1960, Africans line up to get their new passbooks. Many people had publicly burned their passes during a pass-burning campaign. Hundreds now came to collect new passes, without which they could not return to work.

CROSS-REFERENCE
VIOLENCE AND UNREST: PAGES 30–31, 34–35, 36–37, 40–41

South Africa Leaves the Commonwealth

Toward the end of 1960, Verwoerd decided to hold a referendum among white voters to decide whether South Africa should become a republic—without the British queen as the head of state. The result was a narrow majority in favor. It provided the excuse Verwoerd needed to fulfil his next ambition: separation from the Commonwealth of Nations.

DECOLONIZATION

During the late 1950s and early 1960s, the colonial powers gave up many of their colonies. In 1960 alone, 16 African countries gained their independence. The world was changing, and with this change came a new sense of multiracial cooperation. The growing African and Asian membership of the commonwealth felt that South Africa's apartheid policies were unacceptable not only to black South Africans but also to their own dignity. Such policies were clearly out of step with the principle of racial equality that was central to a now multi-racial organization.

DEPARTURE

Hard-line Afrikaners were also eager for South Africa to leave the commonwealth. They believed that it was a hangover from colonialism—in other words, it was a continuation of the British empire by other means.

At a commonwealth meeting in London in March 1961, Verwoerd said South Africa had no desire to leave the organization but was only prepared to remain if members accepted that its apartheid system would not be discussed at commonwealth meetings. Verwoerd's position was strongly opposed by African, Asian, and Canadian delegates. General hostility toward South Africa was also strengthened by the events at Sharpeville and the subsequent declaration of a

In 1960, a group of South African university students take part in a protest against the government's apartheid laws. Although in the minority in their community, many white South Africans who opposed apartheid took part in demonstrations and silent vigils.

TIMELINE

INTERNATIONAL RELATIONS, 1946–1964

1946 ▶ The treatment of South Africa's Indian population is debated at the first meeting of the United Nations (UN).

1952 ▶ The UN sets up a task team to monitor apartheid; the general feeling among its members is that racial segregation in South Africa is a domestic matter.

1960 ▶ As a result of the Sharpeville massacre, the UN attitude toward apartheid becomes more critical.

1960 ▶ Albert Luthuli's efforts to bring about peace in South Africa receive international recognition when he is awarded the Nobel Peace Prize.

1962 ▶ The UN establishes the Special Committee Against Apartheid.

August 1963 ▶ The UN Security Council calls for countries to stop selling arms to South Africa.

1964 ▶ South Africa is excluded from the Olympic Games in Tokyo because of its apartheid regime.

South African prime minister Hendrik Verwoerd arriving in London for commonwealth talks, March 1961.

state of emergency. Rather than face expulsion from the commonwealth, Verwoerd decided to withdraw South Africa from the organization. Returning home, he described the decision to opt out of the commonwealth as a "happy day for South Africa."

CROSS-REFERENCE
SHARPEVILLE: PAGES 22–23
INTERNATIONAL RELATIONS: PAGES 32–33, 36–37 ▶

Condemning apartheid

"We speak out to put the world on guard against what is happening in South Africa. The brutal policy of apartheid is applied before the eyes of the nations of the world. The peoples of Africa are compelled to endure the fact that on the African continent, the superiority of one race over another remains official policy and that in the name of this racial superiority, murder is committed with impunity. Can the United Nations do nothing to stop this?"
Cuban government minister Che Guevara in a speech to the United Nations, December 11, 1964.

Mandela Sentenced to Life Imprisonment

On June 11, 1964, at the end of the Rivonia Trial, eight prominent ANC members, including Nelson Mandela and Walter Sisulu, were sentenced to life imprisonment. They were sent to Robben Island prison. Some of them would remain locked away for a quarter of a century.

UMKHONTO WE SIZWE

By the 1960s, some members of the African nationalist movement had begun to believe that they would never win freedom through non-violent protests. They felt the only way forward was violent resistance. Under the leadership of Nelson Mandela, Umkhonto we Sizwe (the Spear of the Nation) was formed in 1961 to carry out acts of sabotage. Over the following 18 months, it carried out around 200 firebombings, but its activities were halted by the arrest of Mandela in 1962.

RIVONIA

In July 1963, most of the other leaders of Umkhonto were arrested at a farm in Rivonia, near Johannesburg. For 90 days before their trial, police interrogated the men and kept them alone in individual cells. Eventually, 10 of them were brought to trial and charged on four counts: recruiting people to carry out acts of violence, conspiring to commit such acts, communist activities, and requesting and receiving money for these purposes from outside South Africa.

Fully expecting the death sentence, Mandela made a statement at the trial. He defended the ANC's alliance with the South African Communist Party but highlighted the respect he had for the British parliamentary system: "the most democratic in the world." He argued that Umkhonto was an African movement fighting for dignity, for decent livelihoods, and for equal rights.

JUNE 12, 1964

Alongside Nelson Mandela in Robben Island prison was Pan-African Congress leader Robert Sobukwe, shown here in his cell in 1963.

TIMELINE

SOUTH AFRICAN POLITICS, 1960s

1960–1983 ▶ Millions of Africans are forced to move to the Bantustans.

December 1961 ▶ Umkhonto we Sizwe launches a sabotage campaign that involves the firebombing of government offices, post offices, and electricity substations.

June 11, 1964 ▶ Nelson Mandela and seven others are sentenced to life imprisonment.

September 6, 1966 ▶ Hendrik Verwoerd is murdered by an immigrant from Mozambique.

July 21, 1967 ▶ While crossing a railway line, Albert Luthuli is hit by a train and killed.

Robben Island prison

"I could walk the length of my cell in three paces. When I lay down, I could feel the wall with my feet and my head grazed the concrete at the other side. The width was about six feet [1.8 meters], and the walls were at least two feet [60 centimeters] thick. Each cell had a white card posted outside it with our name and our prison service number. Mine read, 'N. Mandela 466/64," which meant I was the 466th prisoner admitted to the island in 1964. I was forty-six years old, a political prisoner with a life sentence, and that small cramped space was to be my home for I knew not how long."

Nelson Mandela, *Long Walk to Freedom* (Little, Brown, 1994).

In 1995, Nelson Mandela returns as a free man to visit the quarry where he endured 12 years of hard labor during his imprisonment on Robben Island.

CROSS-REFERENCE NELSON MANDELA: PAGES 20–21, 40–41, 42–43

The South African Students' Organization

On July 1, 1969, the all-black South African Students' Organization (SASO) was formed under the leadership of Steve Biko. It aimed to bring students together to celebrate their culture and make them aware of their political power. The organization insisted that blacks must lead the fight against apartheid. Although it was in favor of a non-racial society, SASO believed whites should not play a role in achieving that aim.

BLACK CONSCIOUSNESS

For the apartheid regime in South Africa, segregation had unexpected outcomes. The creation of new segregated universities led to a rise in the numbers of African students after 1959. Sending black students to all-black universities (or to segregated classes in "mixed" colleges) resulted in the growth of a movement called Black Consciousness. This was inspired by developments in black religious beliefs and by the Black Power movement in the United States. Black

Consciousness sought to free Africans from the sense of inferiority that resulted from 300 years of white rule. Its aim was to recondition their minds so that they would forcefully demand recognition of their rights.

JULY 1, 1969

Civil rights leader Steve Biko came under a government banning order in 1973 and was put on trial under the Terrorism Act for encouraging student protests at African universities.

STEVE BIKO

SASO leader and Natal University medical student Steve Biko rose to prominence as he worked to

"Black Consciousness seeks to channel the pent-up forces of the angry black masses to meaningful and directional opposition . . . But the type of black man we have today has lost his manhood. Reduced to an obliging shell, he looks with awe at the white power structure and accepts what he regards as the 'inevitable position.'"
Steve Biko. Quoted in Brian Lapping, *Apartheid: A History* (Grafton Books, 1986).

ORGANIZING OPPOSITION, 1960–1975

1960s ▶ Government repression increases—imprisonments and detentions without trial occur regularly.

1970s ▶ Resistance to apartheid increases. Churches and workers organize opposition. Some white people join Africans in the demonstrations.

1971 ▶ The Black People's Convention is set up as a political body organized along Black Consciousness principles.

1975 ▶ The Inkatha Freedom Party (IFP) is founded by Gatsha Mangosuthu Buthelezi, a former member of the ANC Youth League.

coordinate activity between different groups such as the ANC, the PAC, the Natal Indian Congress, and the Coloured Labour Party. He hoped that by working together, these groups could fill the vacuum that was created whenever an organization was banned. He also hoped that as a combined force, they could influence major political parties and create an anti-apartheid presence in the government. Biko criticized the local chiefs of the Bantustans, who had been persuaded to collaborate with the apartheid government to enforce separate development in the largely barren homelands.

CROSS-REFERENCE THE DEATH OF STEVE BIKO: PAGES 32–33

An Inkatha Freedom Party protest. For a short time it appeared that Inkatha and the Black Consciousness movement would work together, but political differences resulted in them pursuing different goals.

The Soweto Uprising

Police and soldiers clash with students protesting against the use of Afrikaans in schools in Soweto, 1976. In the months of rioting that followed, hundreds of people were killed and thousands were injured.

On June 16, 1976, the police fired on a gathering of 15,000 secondary school students in the township of Soweto, near Johannesburg. The students had been protesting against the use of Afrikaans as a teaching language in African schools. The students and their black teachers did not want to exchange ideas in the language of their white rulers.

THE SOUTHWEST TOWNSHIPS

Soweto, short for "south-west townships" had been designed in the 1930s to house black mine workers. Originally, it had provided the most basic accommodation, with no power lines or shopping facilities. The township was gradually improved in the decades that followed, when wide roads and concrete houses were built.

Yet Soweto was still overcrowded, and it was not unusual for between 17 and 20 people to share a four-room house. Forcing students to learn in Afrikaans added to the pressures of life.

A grim warning

"I am writing to you, Sir, because I have a growing nightmarish fear that unless something drastic is done very soon then bloodshed and violence are going to happen in South Africa . . . A people can only take so much and no more . . . A people made desperate by despair and injustice will use desperate means."
In May 1976, Desmond Tutu, the Anglican Bishop of Johannesburg, wrote a letter to the South African prime minister expressing his concerns for peace in the country. Quoted in Brian Lapping, *Apartheid: A History* (Grafton Books, 1986).

AFRICAN EDUCATION, 1975–1976

1975 ▶ The minister of Bantu Education declares that maths and social studies in all African secondary schools must be taught in Afrikaans, even though nearly all the black teachers speak English.

February 1976 ▶ Protests begin over teaching in Afrikaans in Soweto schools.

March 1976 ▶ The Black People's Convention, the South African Students' Organization, and the South African Students' Movement become active in Soweto schools over the issue of schooling in Afrikaans.

May 1976 ▶ School students start boycotting classes in protest.

VIOLENCE

When the police failed to disperse the Soweto crowd with tear gas, they opened fire, killing two people (one of them 13-year-old Hector Pieterson) and injuring many others. The young people scattered and surged through the streets of Soweto, throwing stones and sticks at passing cars and setting fire to buildings. The violence continued for days, with the rioters causing havoc and police responding with bullets, whips, and batons. The uprising triggered riots across South Africa. By the time the rioting subsided several months later, 575 people had been killed (two of them white men who had been stoned to death) and thousands had been injured and arrested.

CROSS-REFERENCE
VIOLENCE AND UNREST:
PAGES 22–23, 34–35, 36–37, 40–41

Schoolchildren chant Black Power slogans on the third day of protests in Soweto, June 1976.

The Death of Steve Biko

On August 18, 1977, South African security police stopped Steve Biko's car at a roadblock. He was taken to a nearby police station for questioning, where, on September 7, he suffered a blow to his head that left him in a coma. After being kept in a cell for three days, unconscious, naked, and shackled, Biko was loaded into the back of a jeep and driven 68 miles (110 kilometers) to a prison hospital in Pretoria. There, on September 12, 1977, he died. He was only 30.

POLICE CUSTODY

In South Africa, deaths in police custody were not unusual. Since 1961, 45 people had died. The police claimed that most of them had either taken their own lives, slipped on bars of soap, or fallen out of windows. However, Biko had influential friends who were not prepared to accept his death as an accident. From around the world, journalists and lawyers came to ask searching questions. Although in the trial that followed no one was called to account for Biko's death, it marked a turning point in South African politics. Some Afrikaners were beginning to have doubts about the wisdom of the apartheid regime, many black people were uniting in powerful opposition to the government, and the world was beginning to take action.

WORLD OPINION

Since 1960, anti-apartheid movements throughout the world had been demanding that big companies and banks stop investing in South Africa. In spite of this, little action was taken. During the 1980s, however, some countries banned the import of South African products, and citizens of many countries put pressure on major companies to pull out of South Africa.

Biko's inspirational leadership and early death made him a martyr—person who had died for his cause. Here mourners chant and demonstrate as they arrive by bus for Biko's funeral in King William's Town in September 1977.

TIMELINE

A SYSTEM UNDER STRAIN, 1974–1985

1974 ▶ As a result of its apartheid policies, South Africa is expelled from the United Nations.

1978 ▶ Banned Black Consciousness organizations get together to form the Azanian People's Organization (AZAPO). AZAPO urges countries of the world to boycott South Africa.

1980s ▶ Organizations and governments around the world launch an international campaign to boycott South Africa.

December 1, 1985 ▶ The Congress of South African Trade Unions (COSATU) is founded, representing 1.8 million workers.

There was also international action against South Africa taking part in sporting events. In the 1970s, wherever South African teams toured, there were large anti-apartheid demonstrations. By the 1980s, many countries and sports bodies had joined a boycott of South African sports, and numerous tours to the country were canceled.

International pressure mounts: in 1976, well-known British actors protest in London against detentions in South Africa.

CROSS-REFERENCE BLACK CONSCIOUSNESS: PAGES 28–29

Trade union activity

In the early 1970s, the gap between black and white wages began to narrow. Between 1970 and 1976, white earnings rose by 3.8 percent, while black earnings increased by 51.3 percent. This was mainly because the manufacturing industry needed more skilled employees, a need that was met by black workers. However, between 1973 and 1976, the economy went into a downturn. The black workforce began to organize into trade unions, and numerous strikes broke out in protest against low wages and bad working conditions. In 1979, the government legalized black trade unions, believing they would be easier to control if they were legal.

Murder in Sharpeville

On September 3, 1984, a protest march over rent increases imposed by the African council in Sharpeville turned into a riot. The protesters viewed the council officials as collaborators who were carrying out the government's repressive policies. When Kuzwayo Jacob Dlamini, the deputy mayor of Sharpeville, opened fire on the protesters, he was stoned to death by the crowd. Six people were sentenced to death for Dlamini's murder, although the sentence was later reduced to life imprisonment.

BOTHA'S REFORMS

By the 1980s, the South African government realized that apartheid had to be reformed to restore foreign investment. Prime Minister P. W. Botha believed that Africans had homelands where they could exercise their rights, but Coloured people and Indians had no homelands and no rights. He therefore gave each of these groups a House, alongside that of whites, in a three-chamber parliament. The proportion of whites to non-whites, however, ensured continued white domination of the political system. Botha's new constitution gave no rights to the African majority. The Coloured and Indian communities did not accept the new constitution and continued to protest alongside the African anti-apartheid movement.

In 1983, white South Africans go to vote in the referendum on Botha's new constitution.

A cloak for apartheid

"The time has come for white people in this country to realize that their destiny is inextricably bound with ours . . . They will never be free as long as they have to lie awake at night worrying whether a black government will one day do to them as they are doing to us . . . To be sure, the new proposals will make apartheid less blatant [obvious] in some ways. It will be modernized and streamlined, and in its multicolored cloak it will be less conspicuous [noticeable] and less offensive to some. Nevertheless, it will still be there."

The Reverend Allan Boesak, addressing a meeting of 10,000 people at Mitchell's Plain township near Cape Town in August 1983 to mark the launch of the United Democratic Front.

TIMELINE

A NEW CONSTITUTION, 1978–1984

September 29, 1978 ▶ P. W. Botha becomes prime minister.

1982 ▶ The National Party splits over Botha's proposed constitutional changes.

August 20, 1983 ▶ The Reverend Allan Boesak launches the United Democratic Front (UDF), an anti-apartheid alliance of churches, civic associations, trade unions, student organizations, and sports groups.

September 3, 1984 ▶ Botha's new constitution offers limited political rights to Coloured people and Indians.

TOWNSHIP UNREST

From Sharpeville, the disturbances spread to many African townships, triggered by a campaign by the newly formed United Democratic Front against Botha's constitution, involving rent boycotts, school boycotts, and strikes. By 1985, it had become the aim of black activists to make the townships "ungovernable." Numerous township councils were overthrown and replaced by unofficial organizations. "People's courts" punished residents accused of being government agents. Black town councilors and policemen, and sometimes their families, were attacked with fire bombs, beaten, and murdered by "necklacing"—placing a gas-filled tire around a person's neck and setting it alight.

CROSS-REFERENCE
VIOLENCE AND UNREST: PAGES 22–23, 30–31, 36–37, 40–41

In 1985, a riot breaks out at a funeral in Duduza township, east of Johannesburg. During this riot, a group of people murdered an African woman accused of helping the police.

State of Emergency

JULY 20, 1985

Under the state of emergency, the South African government used the army and police to suppress resistance in the townships. Here, police officers drive back protesters demanding the release of Nelson Mandela from prison, August 1985.

On July 20, 1985, in response to growing unrest in the townships, the Botha government declared a state of emergency in 36 districts. The government used its emergency powers to impose severe restrictions: it banned many organizations and placed people under house arrest. It restricted people's movements through curfews and detained without trial those it believed to be breaking the law. It used the army, alongside the police, to crush the rebellion. Thousands of people were arrested, interrogated, and tortured.

Sanctions

In the 1980s, the British and US governments, led by Prime Minister Margaret Thatcher and United States President Ronald Reagan, were opposed to sanctions. One reason for this was that during the Cold War (a period of hostility between the United States and the Soviet Union from 1945 to 1988), South Africa had been an ally to the UK and United States because it had supported anti-communist rebels in neighboring African countries. Yet as the world saw the events in the black townships, attitudes began to shift. In 1985, Chase Manhattan, a large New York bank, refused to renew a South African loan. In 1986, the Comprehensive Anti-Apartheid Act was passed in the United States, imposing sanctions against South Africa.

TIMELINE

EMERGENCY MEASURES, 1985–1988

March 21, 1985 ▶ On the anniversary of the 1960 Sharpeville massacre, police open fire on a funeral procession in Uitenhage in the eastern Cape, killing 20 people.

1985 ▶ 2,436 people are detained under the Internal Security Act.

1986 ▶ The Urban Areas Act is repealed, removing pass laws.

August 10, 1987 ▶ 200,000 members of the National Union of Mineworkers begin the longest strike (three weeks) in South African history.

1987 ▶ Slump in the South African economy.

February 24, 1988 ▶ Activities of the UDF and other anti-apartheid organizations are banned.

OPPOSITION AND CENSORSHIP

Despite the government's efforts, hundreds of thousands of Africans who were banned from white-controlled areas ignored the laws and poured into forbidden regions in search of work. Civil disobedience, demonstrations, and other acts of protest increased. On June 12, 1986, the Botha government declared a state of emergency throughout the whole of South Africa. Press and television reporters were prevented from covering violent clashes between protesters and the security forces.

INKATHA AND THE ANC

While much of the violence in the late 1980s and early 1990s was directed at the government, there were also clashes within the African community. Chief Buthelezi was ruler of the KwaZulu homeland in Natal and leader of the Inkatha Freedom Party. He wanted a joint government with the whites for KwaZulu-Natal. The ANC saw this as giving in to the apartheid plan. Many people died in fighting between Inkatha and the ANC. It was later discovered that the government exploited tensions between the two factions and supported one side or the other when it suited it.

Funerals, such as this one for four people killed by police in Port Elizabeth in 1985, soon became political rallying points for opponents of the South African government.

CROSS-REFERENCE VIOLENCE AND UNREST: PAGES 22–23, 30–31, 34–35, 40–41

F. W. de Klerk Is Elected

SEPTEMBER 14, 1989

In 1989, ill health forced P. W. Botha from office. On September 14, F. W. de Klerk was elected as state president. De Klerk soon announced a policy for reform, saying he hoped to create a climate for negotiations that would end apartheid and bring about a new constitution based on the principle of one person, one vote.

A NEW ERA

In his opening address to parliament on February 2, 1990, de Klerk announced changes that would transform the future of South Africa. He repealed the segregation laws and lifted the ban on anti-apartheid groups, such as the ANC. He also announced the release of large numbers of political prisoners, suspended all death sentences, and

The repeal of many segregation laws meant that children could at last be educated in a multiracial environment.

The grain of sand

"'So this,' I thought to myself, 'is Nelson Mandela.' This was the man who, during his twenty-seven years of imprisonment, had become a global icon of the struggle against apartheid. Like a grain of sand trapped in an oyster, Mandela had been a continuous and growing source of irritation to previous governments. Over the years layer after layer of myth—created by our own fears and the adulation of his supporters—had accreted [built up] around him. Now, after twenty-seven years, he and the political realities that he represented had emerged into the full glare of global and national attention."

F. W. de Klerk describes his first meeting with Mandela on December 13, 1989 in his autobiography, *The Last Trek: A New Beginning* (Macmillan, 1999).

TIMELINE

APARTHEID UNRAVELS, 1989–1990

September 1989 ▶ De Klerk announces that protest marches are permitted.

October 15, 1989 ▶ The government releases eight high-ranking political prisoners, including Walter Sisulu.

November 16, 1989 ▶ All public beaches are opened to all races.

December 13, 1989 ▶ De Klerk meets with Nelson Mandela.

February 2, 1990 ▶ The ban is lifted on the ANC, PAC, South African Communist Party, and many other anti-apartheid organizations.

February 2, 1990 ▶ Political prisoners are released, press freedom is restored, and the death penalty is suspended.

June 7, 1990 ▶ The government ends the state of emergency in all provinces except Natal, where fighting persists between the ANC and Inkatha.

lifted the restrictions on the media. Emergency detentions were limited to six months, and people being detained were given access to lawyers and their own doctors.

THE BIGGER PICTURE

In many ways, de Klerk had taken a gamble based on the political situation in the wider world. South Africa was in economic crisis, and foreign sanctions were making matters much worse. If apartheid ended, South Africa would be able to do business again. Also, the dismantling of Communist states in Eastern Europe and the Soviet Union suggested that the ANC and its Communist allies might be weakened and could be controlled if the ban against them was lifted. For de Klerk, the time for negotiating had arrived.

CROSS-REFERENCE
STATE OF EMERGENCY:
PAGES 36–37
ENDING APARTHEID:
PAGES 40–41, 42–43 ▶

With a reputation for patience and tolerance, F. W. de Klerk was a popular National Party leader. His ability to get along with people was invaluable when, as president, he needed support to push through changes that would dismantle the apartheid system.

The Release of Mandela

Here, just after his release, Mandela and his then-wife Winnie raise their fists in the ANC salute to the cheering crowds.

On February 11, 1990, Nelson Mandela was released from prison after 27 years in captivity. In a speech outside the city hall in Cape Town, Mandela thanked all the people and organizations that had campaigned for his release.

NEGOTIATIONS

Over the following two years, the remaining apartheid laws were abolished. The next phase was to extend voting rights to all South African citizens. On May 4, 1990, negotiations started between the ANC and the government, and on August 6, the ANC and Umkhonto we Sizwe announced the end of their armed struggle. On December 20, 1991, the government called together the first Convention for a Democratic South Africa (CODESA) to begin negotiations that would pave the way

Power struggles

"The government was in no great rush to begin negotiations; they were counting on the euphoria that greeted my release to die down. They wanted to allow time for me to fall on my face and show that the former prisoner hailed as a savior was a highly fallible man who had lost touch with the present situation . . . Mr. de Klerk . . . did not make any of his reforms with the intention of putting himself out of power. He made them for precisely the opposite reason: to ensure power for the Afrikaner in a new dispensation. He was not prepared to negotiate the end of white rule."
Nelson Mandela, *Long Walk to Freedom* (Little, Brown, 1994).

TIMELINE

A ROCKY ROAD TO FREEDOM, 1991–1992

1991 ▶ F. W. de Klerk repeals the remaining apartheid laws.

Dec. 20, 1991 ▶ CODESA talks start.

June 17, 1992 ▶ 200 Inkatha militants attack Boipatong.

August 3, 1992 ▶ Mass action by the ANC culminates in a general strike.

September 7, 1992 ▶ ANC members march to Bisho in the Ciskei homeland in the Eastern Cape, which has a history of repression toward the ANC. They are fired on by the Ciskei Defence Force; 29 are killed and 200 injured.

September 26, 1992 ▶ The ANC and government sign the Record of Understanding.

for universal franchise. De Klerk wanted the formal agreement of white South Africans to continue the negotiations. In a whites-only referendum in March 1992, some 69 percent of voters showed their support for the process.

THE BOIPATONG MASSACRE

On the night of June 17, 1992, armed Inkatha members raided Boipatong, a township near Vereeniging, killing 46 people, mostly women and children. The police did nothing to find the criminals. Suspecting government involvement in the attack, the ANC suspended negotiations and for four months concentrated on mass protests. However, after another massacre in Bisho in September, the government and the ANC signed a Record of Understanding in the hope of avoiding further bloodshed. This formed the basis for the transition to a democratic government.

CROSS-REFERENCE NELSON MANDELA: PAGES 20–21, 26–27, 42–43

A scene after the Boipatong killings. The ANC believed that the government and Inkatha were jointly responsible for the killings. Yet Inkatha argued that ANC attacks on its members led it to counter-attack at Boipatong.

The First Non-racial Elections

APRIL 27, 1994

People wait to vote in the momentous April 1994 elections.

On April 27, 1994, voters lined up patiently to cast their votes in South Africa's first multiracial elections. Around 20 million people took part in what Nelson Mandela described as a 'small miracle'—three days of voting that broke with the apartheid past. The United Nations had sent 2,120 international observers to ensure the fairness of the elections. The ANC won 62.6 percent of the national vote, with the National Party winning 20.4 percent and Inkatha 10.5 percent. ANC leaders opted to form a government of national unity with the other two parties.

DIVISIONS AND DISRUPTION

There had also been attempts to disrupt the peace negotiations. Chief Buthelezi of Inkatha objected to the Record of Understanding between the government and the ANC and broke away from the negotiations. The far-right Afrikaner parties opposed the ending of apartheid and threatened to disrupt the process. However, just before the 1994 elections, Inkatha finally agreed to participate, and the far-right groups were not powerful enough to stop the process from proceeding.

THE FIRST BLACK PRESIDENT

On May 10, 1994, Nelson Mandela became South Africa's first black president after almost three centuries of white domination. The inauguration ceremony took place in Pretoria and was attended by politicians and dignitaries from more than 140 countries around the world. The first deputy president was Thabo Mbeki, who would take over the

TIMELINE

THE REBIRTH OF SOUTH AFRICA, 1993–1994

June 3, 1993 ▶ A date is set for South Africa's first non-racial elections.

October 8, 1993 ▶ The UN lifts economic sanctions against South Africa.

October 15, 1993 ▶ De Klerk and Mandela are awarded the Nobel Peace Prize.

November 18, 1993 ▶ An interim constitution is approved.

May 10, 1994 ▶ Nelson Mandela becomes president of South Africa.

June 1, 1994 ▶ South Africa rejoins the Commonwealth.

June 23, 1994 ▶ South Africa reclaims its seat at the UN General Assembly.

Free at last!

"This is one of the most important moments in the life of our country. I stand here before you filled with deep pride and joy—pride in the ordinary, humble people of this country. You have shown such a calm, patient determination to reclaim this country as your own, and now the joy that we can loudly proclaim from the rooftops—Free at last! Free at last! . . . This is a time to heal the old wounds and build a new South Africa."

Nelson Mandela's speech at the ANC celebrations following his election victory, May 2, 1994.

day-to-day business of government, and the second deputy president was F. W. de Klerk.

Yet despite the promise of a new dawn for South Africa, most people had voted along racial lines. Granting everyone a vote did not remove the effects of apartheid; extreme poverty remained a reality for many.

CROSS-REFERENCE
INKATHA: PAGES 36–37
ENDING APARTHEID: PAGES 38–39, 40–41

Nelson Mandela wears the jersey of the South African rugby team, the Springboks, as he congratulates them on their rugby union World Cup victory in 1995. Under apartheid, the Springboks were an all-white team that had been isolated by the international sports community. In 1992, they were readmitted to international rugby.

Hopes for the Future

On October 28, 1998, a report containing the conclusions of the South African Truth and Reconciliation Commission (TRC) was published. The commission had been set up in 1995 to investigate crimes committed under apartheid and bring about some kind of healing. It allowed victims of brutality to tell their stories and others to confess their guilt. The report condemned both the government and the anti-apartheid movement for committing atrocities.

PROBLEMS WITH PROGRESS

In addition to establishing the TRC, Mandela's government of 1994–1999 introduced the Reconstruction and Development Program to try to reduce poverty, but it had limited success. In 1999, Thabo Mbeki became president.

The chairman of the Truth and Reconciliation Commission, Archbishop Desmond Tutu (right), hands over the TRC report to President Mandela in 1998.

He caused international concern when he appeared to deny the growing HIV/AIDS crisis in South Africa and failed to condemn the abusive government of Robert Mugabe in neighboring Zimbabwe. In 2005, Mbeki's deputy, Jacob Zuma, was charged with corruption relating to an arms deal. ANC members who did not agree with the new direction of the government broke away to form a new party, the

Campaigners for the rights of people with HIV/AIDS carry the coffin of a woman who died from the disease at age 31.

TIMELINE

THE CHANGING FACE OF GOVERNMENT, 1999–2009

June 2, 1999 ▶ The ANC wins elections with an increased majority.

December 18, 2007 ▶ Thabo Mbeki loses the race for the ANC presidency to Jacob Zuma.

Sept. 20, 2008 ▶ Mbeki resigns.

Sept. 25, 2008 ▶ Kgalema Motlanthe becomes caretaker (acting) president.

April 6, 2009 ▶ Corruption charges against Zuma are dropped.

May 9, 2009 ▶ Zuma is sworn in as president.

Congress of the People. Black voters' disillusionment with government was reflected in the 2009 election, when the ANC majority was reduced.

THE FUTURE

On May 9, 2009, Jacob Zuma was sworn in as president. He enjoys strong support, especially among trade unionists and the Communist Party, yet he faces major challenges. The worst scenario is that society and the political system break down, and leaders extend their own power at the expense of democracy. The best scenario is that Zuma chooses his advisers wisely to improve the lives of all South Africans.

CROSS-REFERENCE ANC: PAGES 8–9, 18–19, 40–41

Money and politics

"If you gain power in the ANC, it gives you access to other forms of power as well, including economic power. The relationship between money and politics has undermined our political culture . . . Because the ANC is so dominant [in South Africa], it sends the message to people that if they want power, they can gain it through intrigue, and if they succeed, they will, of course, try to retain it through intrigue . . . It becomes clear that after Nelson Mandela left, the office [of president] lost its dignity . . . Will Zuma be able to restore it? Will he able to stay above the fray? I don't know. I hope so."
Johannesburg-based political analyst, Aubrey Matshiqi. Quoted on BBC News website, May 13, 2009.

Key Figures in the Apartheid Era

PIETER WILLEM BOTHA (1916–2006), PRESIDENT OF SOUTH AFRICA

P. W. Botha was prime minister of South Africa from 1978 to 1984, then state president from 1984 to 1989. He strongly supported racial segregation and the apartheid system. In the years leading up to World War II, Botha sympathized with the German Nazi Party but became disillusioned with its politics in the early 1940s. Until 1978, he served under successive South African prime ministers and gained a reputation as a tough, hard working and outstanding administrator. As president, Botha tried to modify apartheid while still maintaining white minority control. His attempts were unsuccessful and were not helped by his uncompromising, often aggressive style. In 1989, he suffered a mild stroke and resigned from office.

FREDERIK WILLEM DE KLERK (1936–), PRESIDENT OF SOUTH AFRICA

F. W. de Klerk was president of South Africa from 1989 to 1994. During the 1970s, he served in the government of P. W. Botha. In 1989, he took over from Botha as leader of the National Party and was elected president later that year. The following year, he opened negotiations with previously illegal anti-apartheid organizations. After the first multiracial elections in 1994, de Klerk was appointed the second deputy president in President Mandela's cabinet. In 1996, de Klerk and other National Party members withdrew from their cabinet posts in order to establish the National Party as an effective opposition to the ANC. In 1997, de Klerk retired from politics.

CHIEF ALBERT JOHN LUTHULI (1898–1967), ANC PRESIDENT GENERAL

Albert Luthuli was president general of the ANC from 1952 to 1960. Born into a Christian Zulu community, Luthuli became a teacher. In 1936, he was elected chief of his community. Christian principles deeply influenced his political style and beliefs for the rest of his life. His public support for the 1952 Defiance Campaign brought him into direct conflict with the South African government. Confined to his home in the country because of banning orders against him, Luthuli wrote speeches for the ANC. He was arrested for treason in 1956 but later released. Luthuli argued consistently for peaceful reform and in 1961 was presented with the Nobel Peace Prize. Yet he was unsuccessful in preventing the ANC's use of more violent tactics from the 1960s on.

NELSON MANDELA (1918–), ANC POLITICAL LEADER AND PRESIDENT OF SOUTH AFRICA

Mandela joined the ANC in 1944 and was one of the leaders charged with treason in 1956. The case against them collapsed in 1961. Mandela was sentenced to life imprisonment in 1963 for his activities as a leading member of Umkhonto we Sizwe and spent the following 27 years in captivity. He was released in 1990 and began working with President F. W. de Klerk to establish a democratic South Africa. The two men were awarded the Nobel Peace Prize in 1993. In 1994, in the first multiracial elections, Mandela was elected president. He backed the establishment of the Truth and Reconciliation Commission to investigate human rights violations during the apartheid era and introduced measures to improve the living standards of the black majority. He retired from office in June 1999.

WALTER ULYATE MAX SISULU (1912–2003), ANC POLITICAL LEADER

Walter Sisulu joined the ANC in 1940 and was responsible for organizing the 1952 Defiance Campaign. By the mid-1950s, Sisulu, along with other leaders, was subjected to increasingly strict police control and banning orders, but he continued in his leadership role. After his acquittal in the Treason Trial in 1961, he joined Umkhonto we Sizwe to continue resistance through a sabotage campaign. In 1963, he was convicted of sabotage and revolutionary activity and imprisoned on Robben Island, where he remained until 1984. He was then transferred to Pollsmoor Prison in Cape Town and released at the end of 1989. In 1991, Sisulu was elected ANC deputy president, and he played a leading role in the negotiations with the National Party over the transition to a multiracial democracy.

OLIVER TAMBO (1917–1993), ANC PRESIDENT

In 1944, Oliver Tambo became secretary of the ANC Youth League. In 1952, he joined Nelson Mandela's law practice to assist African victims of the apartheid laws, and he took an active role in the Defiance Campaign. The following year, Tambo was appointed national secretary of the ANC. In 1955, he helped draft the Freedom Charter; he was arrested for treason but soon acquitted. Following the Sharpeville massacre, Tambo left South Africa to build international support for the South African liberation movement. He became ANC president in 1969 and continued with his work abroad, successfully raising the international status of the organization. He finally returned to South Africa in 1991.

HENDRIK VERWOERD (1901–1966), PRIME MINISTER OF SOUTH AFRICA

Born in the Netherlands, Henrik Verwoerd emigrated to South Africa with his parents as a baby. From 1950, he served in the South African government and became the chief architect of the apartheid system. In 1958, he became prime minister and pushed through many segregationist laws. In 1960, he banned anti-apartheid organizations; the following year, he withdrew South Africa from the Commonwealth. Verwoerd introduced the Bantustan scheme in 1962. In 1966, he was stabbed to death while in parliament.

Glossary

Afrikaner a white South African of mainly Dutch descent

Bantustan another word for "homeland" or "native reserve"; under apartheid, Bantustans were the only areas of South Africa in which black people could own land

boycott organized effort to weaken a country by refusing to trade with it

Ciskei a territory declared to be a self-governing Bantustan in 1972 and reintegrated into South Africa in 1993

civic organization an organization set up to help administer the duties or activities of a town or city

civil disobedience the refusal to obey certain laws as part of a political protest

collaborator someone who assists with an activity or project—the word is often used to describe a person who betrays his or her own group by helping an enemy group

colonist a person who is a founder or inhabitant of a colony (see below)

colony a country ruled by another country as part of its empire

Coloured an apartheid term used to describe people officially classified as mixed race

Commonwealth of Nations a loose alliance of countries that used to be ruled by Britain

communism a political belief system based on ideas developed by Karl Marx, who believed that the state should own all the factories, land, and mines on behalf of the people

communist a follower of communism

compound an enclosure where African workers had to live while working in the mines

concentration camp a camp in which political prisoners are held, usually in very harsh conditions

constitution the system of laws and basic principles by which a state is governed

curfew a rule requiring people to be in their homes at certain times, often at night

democratic describes a political system in which everyone registered has the right to vote (one person, one vote)

discrimination treating people differently and unfairly because of a difference, such as in race, religious beliefs, gender, or age

inauguration a ceremony to mark the admission of a person to office, for example, a president

interrogate to question aggressively

missionary school Christian-run school

nationalist a person who has great pride in his or her country and believes that it should be governed by its own people

non-cooperation refusal to help people in authority by doing what they have asked you to do

pass a document that until 1986 had to be carried by all South African black people over the age of 16; the government used passes to restrict the movement of black people

referendum a vote to decide a single issue

reserve another word for *homeland*

sabotage to destroy or damage equipment, machines, or transportation as a form of protest

sanctions penalties imposed on a country by other countries that may involve economic, financial, and trade boycotts or companies stopping trade with that country

segregation the state of being separate from others; in apartheid South Africa, this meant separation along racial lines

squatter someone who occupies temporary housing, usually on the edge of a city

state of emergency a situation of national danger or disaster in which a government suspends normal law and may restrict freedom

township under apartheid, an urban living area reserved for non-whites

trade union an organization of workers formed to protect and improve their wages and working conditions

universal franchise the right of everyone to vote

Xhosa a group of black African people, most of whom live in the Eastern Cape and speak Xhosa

Further Information

BOOKS
FOR CHILDREN
Cruden, Alex (editor). *Perspectives on Modern World History: The End of Apartheid*. Greenhaven, 2009.

Downing, David. *Witness to History: Apartheid in South Africa*. Heinemann Library, 2005.

Fine, Martin. *Children of Apartheid*. Athena Press Ltd, 2006.

Gogerly, Liz. *Days That Shook the World: The Freeing of Nelson Mandela*. Hodder Wayland, 2005.

Martin, Michael J. *Apartheid in South Africa*. Lucent Books, 2006.

FOR OLDER READERS AND TEACHERS
Brooman, Josh and Roberts, Martin. *South Africa 1948–2000: The Rise and Fall of Apartheid*. Longman, 2001.

Clark, Nancy L. and Worger, William H. *South Africa: The Rise and Fall of Apartheid*. Pearson Education, 2004.

Davenport, T. R. H. *South Africa: A Modern History*. Macmillan, 1992.

de Klerk, F. W. *The Last Trek—A New Beginning*. Macmillan, 1998.

Lapping, Brian. *Apartheid: A History*. Grafton Books, 1986.

Mandela, Brian. *Long Walk to Freedom*. Little, Brown, 1994.

Vandormael, Alain. *Civil Society and Democracy in Post-Apartheid South Africa*. VDM Verlag Dr. Mueller e.K., 2007.

WEBSITES
www.anc.org.za/
African National Congress website, with government information and links to all aspects of the ANC, including historical documents

www.overcomingapartheid.msu.edu/
Firsthand accounts from activists in the anti-apartheid movement

www.sahistory.org.za
South African history site, with timelines and biographies

www.unmultimedia.org/photo/subjects/apartheid.html
Historical images of apartheid in South Africa

Index

Numbers in **bold** refer to photographs.

African National Congress (ANC) 8, 13, 18, 20, 22, 26, 29, 37, 38, 39, 40, 41, 42, 43, 45
Afrikaans 30, 31
Afrikaners 4, **4**, 6, **6**, 7, 11, 14, **15**, 24, 32, 40, 42, 47
ANC Youth League 13, 29
anti-apartheid movement **17**, 20, 22, 23, **24**, 28, 29, 32, 33, **33**, 35, 37 (see also individual groups)
arrests 18, 19, 21, 26, 31, 36
Azanian People's Organization (AZAPO) 33

banning orders 20, 22, 28, 36, 37
Bantu Authorities Act 16, 17, 18
Bantustans 16, 17, 22, 27, 29, 47
Biko, Steve 28–29, **28**, 32, **32**
Black Consciousness 28, 29, 33
Boer Wars 4, 5
Boers (see Afrikaners)
Boesak, Reverend Allan 34, 35
Boipatong 41, **41**
Botha, Louis 7
Botha, P. W. 34, 35, 36, 37, 38, 46
boycotts 18, 25, 31, 32, 33, 35, **43**, 47
Britain 4, 6, 7, 9, 10, 13, 14, 23, 24, 26
Buthelezi, Mangosuthu 29, 37, 42

Cape of Good Hope 4, 5, 6, 7, 9, 10, 37
colonies 4, 5, 6, 24, 47
Coloured people 7, 8, 9, 18, 29, 34, 35, 47
Commonwealth of Nations 24–25, 43, 47
communism 19, 21, 22, 26, 36, 39, 47
compounds 10, **10**, 47
concentration camps 4, **4**, 47
Congress of the People 20–21
Congress of South African Trade Unions (COSATU) 33
constitution 7, 34, 35, 38, 43, 47
Convention for a Democratic South Africa (CODESA) 40, 41

decolonization 24
Defiance Campaign 18–19, **18, 19**
de Klerk, F. W. 38, 39, **39**, 40, 41, 43, 46
detention without trial 29, 36, 37, 39
diamonds 4, **5**
Durban **11**, 12, **14**

economy 22, 33, 37, 39
education 9, 15, 16, **16**, 17, 30–31

elections 8, 11, 14–15, 38, 42, 43, 45

Freedom Charter 20

Gandhi, Mohandas 12, **12**, 13
gold 4, 5, 9, 10
Group Areas Act 15, 16, 18, 21
Guevara, Che 25

Hertzog, J. B. M. 11
HIV/AIDS 44, **44**

Indians 5, 7, 8, 9, 12, **12**, 13, **13**, **14**, 15, 18, 22, 25, 29, 34, 35
Inkatha Freedom Party (IFP) 29, **29**, 37, 39, 41, 42

labor 5, 9, 10, **15**, 17, 22, 33
land 5, 10, 11, 12, 13, 16, 17
laws, apartheid 14–17, 18
    repeal of 37, 38, **38**, 39
Luthuli, Albert 19, 20, 21, 25, 27, 46

Macmillan, Harold 23
Malan, Daniel 11, 14, **15**, 18
Mandela, Nelson 13, 19, 20, 21, 26, 27, **27**, 38, 39, 40, **40**, 42, 43, **43**, 44, **44**, 45, 46
map of South Africa **6**
Mbeki, Thabo 42, 44, 45
Milner, Lord Alfred 7
mining 5, **5**, 7, 9, 10, **10**, 15, 37

Natal 6, 10, 12, 28, 37, 39
Natal Indian Congress (NIC) 12, **13**, 29
National Party 11, 23, 35, 42
Native Urban Areas Act 11
Natives' Land Act 9, 10–11
Nobel Peace Prize 25, 43
non-violent resistance 12, 13

Orange Free State 6, 8, 10
Orange River valley 4

Pan-African Congress (PAC) 22, 29, 39
passbook burning 9, 18, **19**
Passive Resistance Campaign 12–13
pass laws 7, 8, 9, 12, 16, 18, 19, 22, **23**
police 12, 21, 22, **22**, 26, 30, **30**, 31, 32, 35, 36, **36**, 37, 41
    deaths in police custody 32

Record of Understanding 41, 42
reform of apartheid 34, 38, 39, 40
reserves 10, 11, 17, 47
riots **14**, 15, 31, 34, 35, **35**

Rivonia Trial 26
Robben Island prison 26–27, **26, 27**

sabotage 26, 27, 47
sanctions 36, 39, 47
schools 4, 9, 16, **16**, 17, 20, 30, 31
segregation 10, 11, 12, 15, 17, 19, 22, 25, 28, 38, 47
Sharpeville massacre 22, **22**, 24, 25, 37
    riots 34–35
Sisulu, Walter 13, 26, 39, 46
Smuts, Jan 4, 7
Sobukwe, Robert 13, **26**
Sophiatown 21, **21**
South African Communist Party (SACP) 9, 19, 26, 39, 45
South African Native Affairs Commission 7
South African Native National Congress (SANNC) 8, **8**, 9
South African Students' Organization (SASO) 28, 31
Soweto Uprising 30–31, **30, 31**
squatting 16, 17, 47
state of emergency 22, 25, 36–37, 39, 47
strikes 9, **9**, 15, 18, 33, 35, 37, 41
students **24**, 28–29, 30, **30**, 31

Tambo, Oliver 13, 21, 46
townships 11, 22, 35, **35**, 36, **36**, 41, **41**, 47 (see also Sharpeville and Soweto)
trade unions 9, 11, 33, 37, 45, 47
Transvaal 4, 6, 7, 10, 12
Treason Trial 21
Truth and Reconciliation Commission (TRC) 44
Tutu, Desmond 30, **44**

Umkhonto we Sizwe 26, 27, 40
Union of South Africa 6–7, 8
United Democratic Front (UDF) 34, 35, 37
United Nations (UN) 25, 33, 42, 43
universities 17, 28

Vereeniging, Peace of 4
Verwoerd, Hendrik 16, 17, 22, 23, 24, 25, **25**, 27, 46
voting rights 7, 8, 15, 20, 34, 38, 40, 41, 42, **42**, 43

women 9, 23

Zuma, Jacob 44, 45